Wing Chun Kung-fu: A Complete Guide

VOLUME THREE

Weapons and Advanced Techniques

CHINESE MARTIAL ARTS LIBRARY

WING CHUN KUNG-FU

VOLUME THREE

Weapons & Advanced Techniques

Dr. Joseph Wayne Smith

CHARLES E. TUTTLE CO., INC.
Rutland, Vermont & Tokyo, Japan

Acknowledgments
I am grateful to Kathelene Tollenaar for taking the photographs for the
three volumes in this series and to Ina Cooper for word processing.

Published by the Charles E. Tuttle Publishing Co., Inc.
of Rutland, Vermont & Tokyo, Japan
with editorial offices at
1-2-6 Suido, Bunkyo-ku, Tokyo 112

LCC Card No. 92-80690
ISBN 0-8048-1720-0

First edition, 1992
Second printing, 1993

PRINTED IN SINGAPORE

Contents

Introduction

This is the third and final book in my complete guide to Wing Chun kung-fu. The broad aim of this project has been to present a concise, systematic, and scientific analysis of the Wing Chun system, which although condensed will be informative not only to Wing Chun practitioners, but to other martial artists as well. To do this has involved deconstructing the system and breaking through the curtain of secrecy, mysticism, and controversy surrounding the art. As I pointed out in the introduction to volume two of this series, there is often great vagueness about why Wing Chun skills are as they are, and why techniques do or do not work. There is even less room in traditional martial arts for scientific and logical criticism of techniques or experimentation. This has led some martial artists to abandon classical systems altogether and adopt eclectic freestyle systems. However, apart from some outstanding freestyle contributions, typically devised for advanced martial artists, the baby is often tossed out with the bath water, leaving one with the silt of often incongruous techniques and contradictory approaches that lack functional harmony. This three-volume treatise has dealt with this philosophical problem of the martial arts by advocating a middle way—to think about a traditional martial art such as Wing Chun kung-fu in a non-classical way. Accordingly, certain core historical and cultural aspects of the art have been retained, but in order to be scientifically oriented, there must be room for modifications in the light of experience.

Volume one in this series, *Basic Forms and Principles*, gave a comprehensive analysis of the building blocks of the Wing Chun system, namely the three forms—*Sil Lum Tao, Chum Kil,* and *Bil Jee.* That book defined terms, outlined the meaning of specific body movements, and summarized the key principles of Wing Chun kung-fu. The second volume, *Fighting and Grappling,* studied Wing Chun strategy or logistics, explaining how to fight using the Wing Chun empty-hand and foot techniques in realistic combat situations. This involved a study of the fighting skills of Wing Chun, including sticky-hands, sticky-legs, *chin-na,* and the poison-touch theory of vital strikes to the weak points of human anatomy *(dar mak).* In this book I discuss, and photographically illustrate the wooden-dummy form and its combat applications, as well as the butterfly knives and the six-and-a-half pole form. Attempting to outline both the wooden-dummy form and its applications as well as the Wing Chun butterfly knives in one volume is a tall order. Consequently this book, following the trend set by the previous two volumes, has no padding but attempts to get down to the meat of the matter. Because the books have been written in a progressive and systematic fashion, it is hoped that the student will purchase all three volumes in this series. However, a detailed glossary has been included explaining important terms used in the previous two volumes.

In my previous books I spent considerable time in textual discussion dealing with martial-art controversies to clean-up conceptual messes and confusions. This book builds upon that foundation. The chapter discussions are briefer because there are fewer controversies regarding the Wing Chun weapons. Differences between the Wing Chun styles in this respect are largely differences in the organization of the forms or katas, rather than in the assembled techniques. Again, my concern is to present a clear and logical outline of the relevance of the moves from the forms and their combat applications. I attempt to present in this volume Wing Chun weapons forms that are sensible and rational. As the reader will see, my presentation is completely consistent with the Wing Chun philosophy adopted in my previous books. The Wing Chun weapons are an extension of the empty-hand forms, not radically different forms haphazardly welded onto the Wing Chun system. Therefore both the empty-hand forms and the weapons forms must constitute an organic unity; a coherent and functional whole, the parts of which fit naturally together and mutually interact and support each other.

Furthermore, consistent with my apolitical position, I must add that I do not have any desire to enter into debates about which are the authentic Wing Chun weapons forms that have been passed down from the sacred mountain of martial-art knowledge by the messengers of the gods if not by the gods themselves! These debates about origins are incapable of scientific or historical resolution as the primary data is typically not available for scrutiny, and what is available is usually controversial in itself. My concern again, is only with that which is a rational and scientific aid to effective combat and self-defense.

It is my aim to show that in the age of the gun, the Wing Chun weapons are still relevant for an overall self-defense education in combat arts—not only as weapons in themselves, but also through the more general combative principles embodied in their use and the many physical benefits derived from training with them.

1

The Wooden-Dummy Form

THE POINT OF THE WING CHUN WOODEN-DUMMY

The Wing Chun wooden-dummy is a symbolic training tool. It consists of a thick round post mounted on a supporting frame that allows the post to vibrate to some degree when struck. From the top part of the dummy two smooth arms protrude and another single arm protrudes from the middle. These arms represent high- and middle-range attacks. There is also a forward leg with a bend in it which represents the knee of the forward leg. The lower stem of the dummy represents the back leg.

The Wing Chun wooden-dummy form concludes the empty-hand forms of Wing Chun. It may be wondered why an entire form, especially an advanced one, should be based upon a training tool? It is because there are a number of benefits that can be derived from wooden-dummy training, such as:

1. The use of a dummy that can be struck adds realism to training and a dummy is hardier than a training partner!

2. The dummy form can improve *chi sao* as the movements of the form involve sticky-hands and not the violent banging of the dummy arms. The dummy is not the best possible conditioning tool for toughening the arms. Rather it is a convenient way to practice the smooth transition between hand forms as well as the application of inch-force to hand strikes such as the palm-strike.

3. This form contains more kicks than the *Chum Kil* form; it may be called Wing Chun's kicking form.

4. There are many excellent sequences of techniques in the form that can be extracted and applied in combat.

5. Above all, the wooden-dummy form is a way of training footwork. Too often, concentration is focused upon the hand movements of the form without much thought being paid to entry techniques or how to get in and out of an opponent's guard.

ANALYSIS OF THE WOODEN-DUMMY FORM

Section One. The first section of the wooden-dummy form opens with some subtle moves. There is a lift of the left hand typically used as a defense against fast jabs. This is followed by a right palm-strike through the center-line and a thumb gouge that symbolically represents an eye gouge. From this, the neck-pulling technique follows. In the form, the dummy's arm is pulled and its neck jerked down. In real combat, an opponent's neck is pulled down upon a punch.

Apart from the above techniques, one other important technique in section one of the wooden-dummy form is the following sequence: against a straight punch, defend with a rear *bong sao,* then take a step forward moving the lead leg first approximately 45 degrees to the opponent's center-line and then walk into the side of the opponent, maintaining contact with his attacking arm at all times, locking up his leg with what was previously your back leg. The *bong sao* is glued to his arm, and then changes to a *taun sao* as you move and strike the head or body. This type of footwork illustrates perhaps one of the most important fighting principles of Wing Chun: attempt to get into an opponent on his side, lock up his leg, press on one arm, and use his body to block the use of his other arm.

Section Two. This section is identical to section one, except that it is performed first on the right-hand side, so that both the hand positions and the footwork are reversed.

Section Three. This is a very rich section containing many excellent techniques. The section opens with three parries. These are of interest because they do not involve moving the entire arm in parrying, but only the wrist. The use of the entire arm in parrying theoretically leaves the center-line momentarily open, which is a weakness. After the last wrist parry, an ordinary parry is performed with a 90-degree pivot and chop. Then the arm is drawn down and a punch is forced into the opponent's abdomen at solar plexus level. The next important technique is unique in the Wing Chun system. You step in at an angle as in sections one and two, only this time step in with the right foot, leaving the left stationary, and deliver a body chop with the right hand while parrying with the left. This means that for an instant you are in quite a wide stance. After springing in to deliver an attack, move out by moving only the right leg back. As a simultaneous defense and attack, a heel-kick to the side of the opponent's body is launched by the right foot and a wrist-flicking *bong sao* is delivered with the right arm. This *bong sao* has as its primary purpose the defense of the head, but like so many Wing Chun hand moves it also has an offensive use: the flicking fingers of the *bong sao* are directed toward the opponent's eyes. This sequence of movements is repeated on the right-hand side of the dummy with an exchange of the hands and kicking leg.

Section Four. This is a complicated form with a simple training purpose. The bulk of the hand moves in this form are concerned with moving around the opponent's guard, opening it up, and striking. The opening movement for example, consists of a double *taun sao* with both arms outside the dummy's arms and a double *haun sao* to get into its center-line, followed by a double palm-strike to the solar plexus, and a double palm-strike to the face. Both palm-strikes are delivered with inch-force; that is, they are jarring strikes. In addition, the sequence of *bong sao* and *taun sao* performed on the top two arms is an excellent way of developing the ability to swim your hands around an opponent's guard.

Another kick occurs in this section. This time, in moving to the left, you perform a right *taun sao*, left palm-strike, and right knee kick. This is repeated, but reversed on the right-hand side of the dummy.

Section Five. The theme of this section is the use of the double palm-strike. As can be seen from the photographs, the double palm-strike can be used for an attack on both the inside and outside position. When on the inside, the opponent's guard is forced open for a strike. When on the outside, the opponent's guard is closed up and the double palm-strike is forced over the top of the guard.

There are two other important movements in this section that merit discussion. In the opening section, there is another example of the economical use of the wrist in deflecting punches. Here the hand is held like a snake ready to strike, the fingers together and straight, the palm down, and the wrist slightly bent. Deflection occurs by moving the wrist from side to side, like a snake moving its head. This is a very safe form of deflection that does not endanger one's own center-line and that allows a ready strike with the fingertips.

Following the above move, there is a new type of *bong sao*, a downward brush, or scoop-away, *bong sao*. The idea behind this technique is to get your palm on the top of a straight punch and then to pat it down and away. As this is done, the body pivots to the side so that your body is 'outside' of the punch and so that the punch can sail past, while you retaliate with a punch or palm-strike. This is a good defense technique to use against chest level punches.

Section Six. Two new skills are introduced in this section; both skills are very simple but surprisingly effective. The first is a defense against a straight punch. Defend against the punch with a *bong sao*, pivoting to your side. If the opponent is facing you and punches with his right hand, pivot so that you face your left and perform a right *bong sao*. Now simultaneously pull the attacking arm down with the hand which previously formed a defensive *bong sao*, as you chop with your other arm and simultaneously pivot back. Chances are that the pivot and pull alone will throw the opponent to the floor, while the chop to the throat is a finishing technique.

In this section, there is also a variation upon the kicking and grabbing skill seen in section four. This time, however, the kick is to the knee of the back leg; usually, a kick to the back of the knee is used to put the opponent on the floor when the body weight is concentrated on the back leg.

Section Seven. This section adds further kicking skills to the Wing Chun system. The section begins with a right *taun sao* against an imaginary straight punch, and a left heel kick to the groin. The left hand is then raised into a *bong sao* defense as the left foot stamps on the knee. The knee on the opponent's lead leg is usually attacked. A stamping kick is a low kick that involves allowing your body weight to fall through a kick. This in itself makes this kick the most powerful low kick in the system. However, further power is added to this kick by pulling the opponent onto the kick. This technique is also seen in section eight.

Also featured in section seven is a skill from sticky-leg (*chi gerk*) fighting. Walk close to the dummy and slip your right foot behind the front dummy leg, parrying the dummy hand. The heel is raised off the ground but the toes are on the ground. Then simultaneously palm-strike the chest of the dummy and flex the right calf muscle backward. This is a typical Wing Chun throwing technique. Here, as in all parts of Wing Chun, emphasis is placed upon balance by keeping at least part of both feet on the ground. If you were to lift your right leg off the ground, at precisely that instant you would be vulnerable to a counter-throw.

Section Eight. The concluding section of the wooden-dummy form also features some excellent techniques. The first is the opening move, which involves the chicken-wing *bong sao*. We first saw this type of *bong sao* in the *Chum Kil* form. In this section, the chicken-wing *bong sao* is used to deflect a lower body attack, typically a straight punch or linear kick. This is done by the skillful use of pivoting to harmlessly redirect the force of the attack rather than to meet it full on; it is never advisable to use hard force against a potentially harder force. To cover the upper body from an attack, a *taun sao* sweeps up, and after redirecting an attack, a palm-strike is delivered in one fluid movement.

However, the most noteworthy technique in this form is the following technique: against a straight punch, defend with a high side *bong sao* as in the *Chum Kil* form. Now jerk the opponent down, pulling him forward with the force of both your arms, and simultaneously kick the opponent's knee. The receiving knee not only suffers the force of the kick, but the violent jerk forward jackknifes the opponent's own body against his knee joint.

This technique is a symbol of the sort of fighting skills found in Wing Chun kung-fu. The system, as we have shown, is a no-nonsense system especially designed for street fighting survival, and the wooden-dummy training form is an important aspect of this training. In these violent days, when ordinary citizens are beaten up, robbed, and raped, I hope that with respect to unarmed self-defense, my discussion helps someone survive a violent attack.

1   2   3

THE WOODEN-DUMMY FORM

Note: to avoid needless repetition of sequenced photographs which would complicate an already long and difficult form, some photographs of movements which are constantly repeated are deleted after their initial appearance, and a reference note made. This makes it possible to take in each section with the eye and select the most important moves for study. The glossary should be referred to in conjunction with the following instructions. All references to "taking a step" or "stepping," refer to elementary Wing Chun footwork, described in volume one, whereby a step is taken with the lead foot, with the rear foot being slid along the ground to maintain the stance and balance in close-range combat.

SECTION ONE

1. Facing the dummy as shown, standing in the parallel stance, lift the top left dummy arm with a rising palm-strike and deliver a right palm-strike to the head area of the dummy.

2. Now, simultaneously pivot to the left 90 degrees, pull the top dummy arm with your left hand, and grasp the neck while gouging with your right thumb to eye level. This is the eye-gouge technique.

3. Then deliver a right *bong sao* before stepping.

4   5   6

7   8

4. Now take a step and then pivot 90 degrees and walk into the dummy as shown, simultaneously delivering a left palm-strike to the ribs and defending with a right *taun sao*. Lock up the dummy's leg with your right leg.

5. Then take a step back from the dummy, moving to the right. Perform a left *taun sao* to the top arm and right *gaun sao* with your right arm.

6. Then before stepping, perform a left chicken-wing *bong sao* or low *bong sao* with a right *taun sao*.

7. Take a step to the right and then step in close to the dummy, performing a left *taun sao* and right palm-strike to the ribs. The hand moves are coordinated with the second step such that the step is used to add momentum to the hand attacks. Unless indicated otherwise, all dummy techniques are performed in this way so that footwork maximizes the force behind hand attacks.

9

10

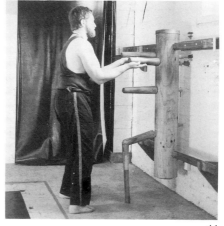

11

8. Now deliver a concluding right *taun sao* to the middle arm and left *gaun sao* to the lower arm. This move is repeated many times in the form.

9. Step away from the dummy and return to the start position as shown in Figure 1. Draw in the dummy arms by locking onto or sticking to the arms and pulling them towards you (*see* the *Sil Lim Tao* form in volume one), and deliver a right palm-strike as in Figure 1.

10. Now draw in both of the dummy arms.

11. Then conclude section one of the form with the double lifting hands. The movements in Figures 8-11 are repeated many times in the form and will henceforth be referred to as the concluding movements. Return to the basic *Sil Lum Tao* parallel stance, in guard position.

12   13   14

SECTION TWO

This section is exactly like section one of the form only you pivot to the right-hand side initially, and then step to the right around the dummy. This section is performed by simply repeating all of the moves seen above, this time on the right-hand side and by reversing the order of left and right hands in the respective moves. For example, the opening neck pull is now done with the left hand and on the right-hand side, and so on.

Section two of the dummy form concludes exactly as the first section of the form.

SECTION THREE

12. Deliver a right palm-strike to the top dummy arm from the parallel stance.

13. Then a left palm-strike to the middle dummy arm.

14. Then another right palm-strike to the top dummy arm.

15. Now pivot on the spot to the right 90 degrees and deliver a left parry to the top dummy arms.

16. Follow this up with a left chop to the face section of the dummy.

17. Then pivot back 90 degrees to the front-on position. Draw in

15 16 17

18 19 20

the top dummy arm with your left hand. Punch with your right arm
to the dummy's chest.

18. Immediately pivot on the spot 90 degrees to the left and deliver
a right parry to the outer surface of the middle dummy arm.

19. Now pivot 90 degrees back to the front-on position and deliver
a right hand chop to the face section of the dummy.

20. Again, draw in the middle dummy arm with your right hand.
Punch to the dummy's chest level with your left hand.

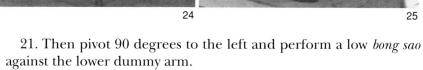

21. Then pivot 90 degrees to the left and perform a low *bong sao* against the lower dummy arm.

22. Take a step to the left, pivot 90 degrees and face the dummy. Prepare to spring in and perform a parry and chop. The spring should be an explosive movement, moving the right foot in to lock up the dummy leg, whilst keeping the left foot stationary for a retreat. This wide stance is maintained only for an instant, solely to deliver a quick attack and a speedy retreat.

23. Now deliver the left parry to the top arm and chop to the ribs of the dummy.

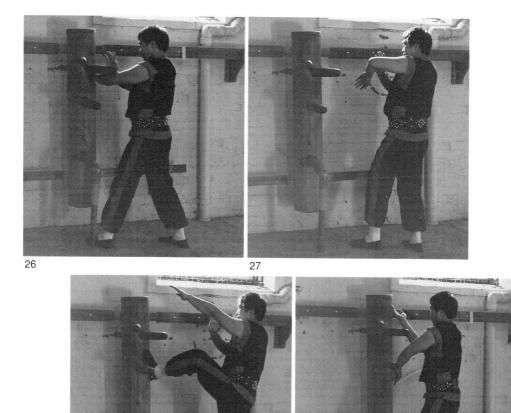

26

27

28

29

24. Follow this up with a heel kick and a high right flicking *bong sao* to defend your head.

25. Then step right, parallel to the dummy and perform a low *bong sao* with your left arm.

26. Perform a right parry and left chop.

27. Step back and guard yourself with a *bong sao*.

28. Now, as before, deliver a heel kick and flicking *bong sao*.

29. Then repeat the concluding moves exactly as in section one to conclude this section of the form.

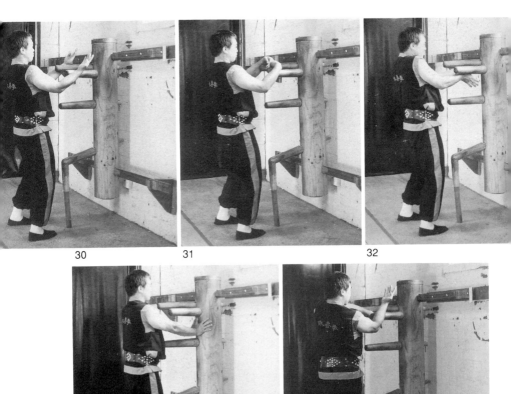

30   31   32

33   34

SECTION FOUR

30. Deliver a double *taun sao* with both arms outside the respective dummy arms.

31. Then perform *haun sao* around the dummy arms by curling your hands from outside of the dummy arms to the inside position. This symbolizes getting inside an opponent's guard position.

32. Now prepare to deliver a double palm-strike below the dummy arms.

33. Deliver the double palm-strike to the chest level of the dummy.

34. Now pivot 90 degrees to the left. Then perform a left *bong sao*

35

36

37

38

and right *taun sao* to the higher and middle dummy arms respectively. Pivot 90 degrees back to face the dummy front on. Maintain contact with the dummy arms.

35. Then pivot 90 degrees to the right. Now perform a left *taun sao* and right *bong sao* to the higher and middle dummy arms respectively. The arms flow around the dummy arms.

36. Pivot 90 degrees back to the front-on position. Again draw in the dummy arm. Prepare for a right palm-strike. Control the upper arm of the dummy with your left through light contact.

37. Then deliver a right palm-strike to the dummy's head.

38. Now pivot 90 degrees to the left, and perform a right *bong sao* to the high dummy arm.

39   40

39. Now, whilst maintaining contact with the dummy arm, take a step with your lead foot to a position approximately 45 degrees clockwise from the dummy's center-line (as shown), and prepare to step into the dummy for a closer attack. Immediately change from a *bong sao* to a *taun sao*, sliding around the dummy arm. Simultaneously deliver a palm-strike with the left hand and a right front-foot heel-kick to the dummy's knee.

40. Then step back from the dummy, and facing right, perform a left-hand *taun sao* to the high dummy arm and a right-hand *gaun sao* to the low dummy arm.

Now repeat the above sequence of movements, reversing the left and right hands, on the other side. Repeat the movements in Figures 36 to 39 and finish with the concluding movements from section one.

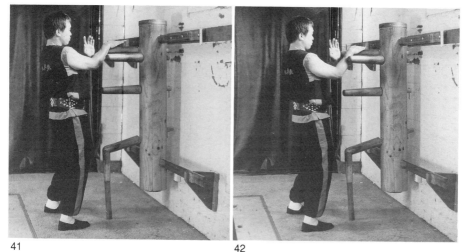

41   42

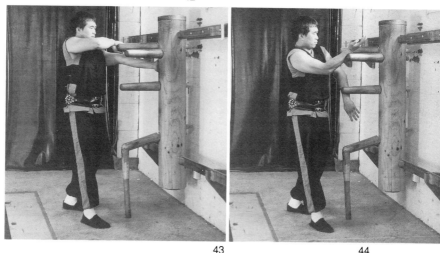

43   44

SECTION FIVE

41. From the parallel stance deliver a forearm deflection to the upper dummy arm with your right forearm.

42. Then deliver the same forearm deflection to the middle dummy arm.

43. Now, pivoting 90 degrees clockwise, deliver a scooping or patting down *bong sao* with the right hand and palm-strike to the ribs with the left hand.

44. Then, still facing right, perform a right *taun sao* and left low *bong sao*.

45

46

47

45. Pivot 90 degrees to the front-on position and deliver a double palm-strike (right hand on top, left below) through the center-line. The fingers touch the target, momentarily maintaining contact, before delivering a powerful jolt.

46. Now, after pivoting 90 degrees to the right and taking a step, step in with the left foot close to the dummy and deliver another double palm-strike (left hand on top, right below).

47. Then step back from the dummy slightly and perform the right *taun sao* and left *gaun sao* as shown. Return to the center front-on position and repeat the previous move of the double palm-strike through the center-line. Then pivot 90 degrees to the left and take a step with the lead foot.

48

49

48. Now step into the dummy as you have done previously and deliver another double palm-strike followed by *taun sao* with left hand on high dummy arm and *gaun sao* with right hand on low dummy arm.

49. Now return to the center front-on position. Draw in dummy arm on the right and palm-strike on the left. Conclude the section as seen previously in Figures 8 to 11.

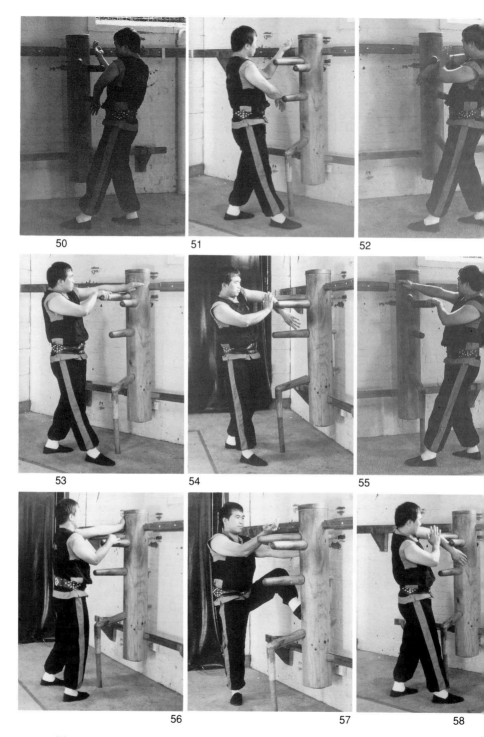

50

51

52

53

54

55

56

57

58

59

SECTION SIX

50. Pivot 90 degrees anticlockwise, performing *gaun sao* and *taun sao*.

51. Then pivot 180 degrees clockwise, performing *taun sao* and *gaun sao* and return to the position in Figure 50.

52. Immediately follow up with a *bong sao* to the top dummy arm.

53. Now pivot 180 degrees clockwise, grab the high dummy arm with your right hand and chop to the dummy face with your left.

54. Then perform a *bong sao* against the middle dummy arm.

55. Now pivot 180 degrees anticlockwise, repeating the grab-and-chop technique.

56. Pivot 90 degrees to the center front-on position, draw in the middle dummy arm and deliver a left palm-strike to the side of the dummy's face. Then pivot 90 degrees to the left, perform the *bong sao* to the high dummy arm with the right arm.

57. Now use a right *taun sao* to defend against the high dummy arm, whilst simultaneously delivering a back foot heel-kick and left palm-strike.

58. Now, stepping right, perform a left *bong sao* on the middle dummy arm.

59. Now as previously seen, deliver the *taun sao*, palm-strike and back foot heel-kick again.

Conclude this section with the concluding movements of section one.

60

61

62

SECTION SEVEN

60. From the center front-on position deliver a right *taun sao* to the middle dummy arm.

61. Now from the center front-on position immediately launch a left foot heel-kick to the groin region of the dummy.

62. Then simultaneously withdraw the *taun sao* and form a defensive *bong sao* with your left arm and deliver a left stomping-kick to the dummy's knee.

Return then to the parallel stance in the center front-on position. Repeat the above sequence using the opposite hands and legs.

63

64

65

66

63. Then pivot left 180 degrees, performing a low *bong sao* with the right arm to the lower dummy arm.

64. Move into the dummy, deliver a palm-strike and *Bil Jee* leg sweep.

65. Moving right, repeat the low *bong sao* with left arm.

66. Repeat the palm-strike and leg sweep, this time on the right hand side.

Conclude the section with the concluding movements from section one.

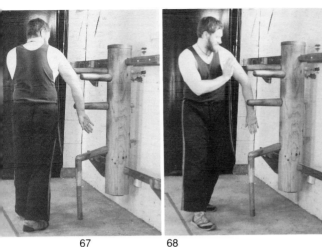

67   68   69

70   71   72

SECTION EIGHT

67. Pivot 90 degrees to the left, deliver a right-arm low *bong sao* in a swinging fashion.

68. Then pivot 180 degrees to the right, deliver a left-arm low *bong sao* also in a swinging fashion.

69. Repeat the low *bong sao* after pivoting 180 degrees to the left.

70. Return to the center front-on position by pivoting. Perform a right *taun sao* to the middle dummy arm.

71. Then launch a right palm-strike to the dummy's face.

72. Repeat the series of low *bong saos* done previously: left hand low *bong sao* then right and left again.

73   74   75

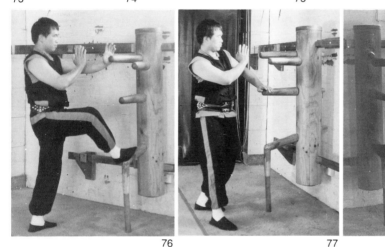

76   77   78

73. Return to the center front-on position. Left *taun sao* performed against high dummy arm.

74. Then launch a left palm-strike to the dummy's face.

75. Now pivot 90 degrees to the left and do a *gum sao* or downward depressing palm-strike.

76 Take a step. Then parry the top dummy arm with your left hand and deliver a right-foot heel-kick.

77. Stepping to the right, repeat the *gum sao* or downward depressing palm-strike.

78. Then repeat the parry and knee kick, this time on the right-hand side of the dummy.

79   80   81

82   83

79. Now, moving left, repeat the *gum sao,* followed by a *bong sao* to the upper dummy arm.

80. Then perform a double hand-grab and knee kick. Step right and perform another high *bong sao.*

81. Now repeat the double hand-grab and knee kick.

82. Return to the center front-on position by stepping down and pivoting. Draw in both of the dummy's arms.

83. Conclude the form with the double lifting action.

84   85

86   87

COMBAT APPLICATIONS OF THE
WOODEN-DUMMY FORM

84. The larger fighter throws a left punch.

85. The smaller fighter deflects the punch with a *taun sao*, simultaneously locking up and sticking to the legs and delivering a palm-strike to the ribs.

86. Then a finishing blow is delivered: a palm-strike under the chin.

87. Again, against a straight punch the larger fighter defends with a *til sao*. The punching arm can now be readily grabbed.

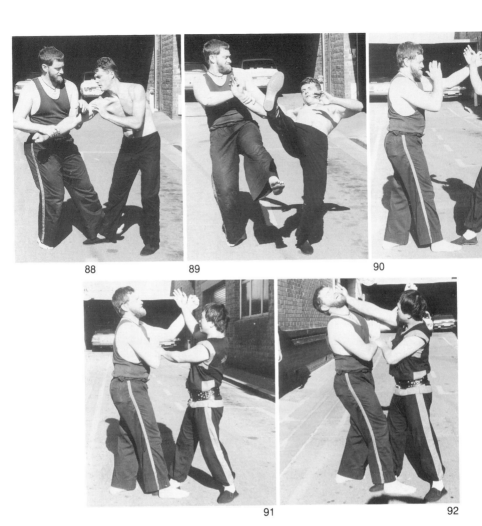

88
89
90

91
92

88. The punching arm is now grabbed and locked in an arm-bar. The smaller fighter's foot is also locked up in preparation for a sticky-leg technique.

89. The smaller fighter's right foot is now swept, whilst his arm is jerked in the opposite direction, ending the attack.

90. The larger fighter delivers a straight punch, which the smaller fighter neutralizes with a *til sao* or lifting hand.

91. Then the larger fighter's right arm is pinned, whilst the smaller fighter sticks to the larger fighter's left arm.

92. Having gained the center-line position a palm-strike to the chin is delivered.

93. The larger fighter has thrown a very risky double roundhouse

93   94

95   96

punch, which is met by a double *taun sao* from the inside position. The same defense could also be used against a lunge for the throat.

94. Then the smaller fighter counterattacks with double palm-strikes to the face, followed up with double eye-gouges by the thumbs.

95. The larger fighter again delivers a straight left punch. This is responded to by a grab-and-chop to the throat. Notice the failed *taun sao* which has been too slow in defense of the chop.

96. This is then followed up by an arm trap, performed by pulling the failed *taun sao* of the larger fighter. Then a cutting palm-strike to the jaw follows. This could very well constitute a knock-out blow.

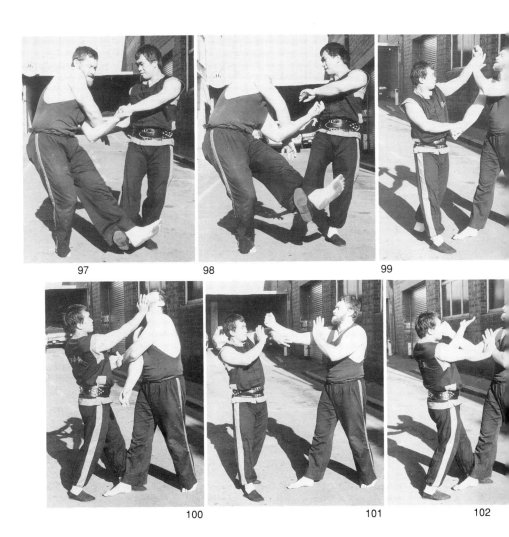

97

98

99

100

101

102

97. The larger fighter's leg is then lifted using sticky-legs, whilst the arm is jerked violently.

98. A throw sideways is then attempted.

99. Here the larger fighter uses the lifting hand move, or a *til sao* to defend against the smaller fighter's grab and back fist.

100. The smaller fighter then grabs the larger fighter's defensive hand, traps the hands, and delivers a rising palm-strike to the chin.

101. The larger fighter throws a straight punch which the smaller fighter defends against with a *bong sao*.

102. Then the smaller fighter, whilst still sticking to the larger

103   104   105

106   107

fighter's arm changes the *bong sao* to a *taun sao* to open up the center-line and traps the opponent's rear hand.

103. Now there is a clear shot at the jaw, and a cutting palm-strike is delivered, ending the attack.

104. Again the larger fighter throws a straight punch, which is once more deflected by the smaller fighter's *bong sao*.

105. This is responded to by a 180-degree pivot, arm grab, and chop.

106. Another grab and pivot traps the arms. Then an eye-gouge or rip is performed.

107. Then this is followed up by pulling the larger fighter's throat onto a *bil jee* or finger thrust, ending the attack.

108   109

110   111

108. Against a straight punch, a *taun sao* and palm-strike may be used to attack the top gate of an opponent, whilst a stomping kick to the back of the knee is delivered.

109. The stomping kick has not injured the larger fighter's knee, but it has destabilized him.

110. The larger fighter is then controlled by the *chin-na* skills explained in volume two; in this case an arm bar applying pressure to the elbow joint by bending it back against its natural angle of motion. This ends the attack.

111. Now the two fighters square off.

112. The smaller fighter then throws a straight punch which is deflected by the larger fighter's *bong sao*. The larger fighter has

112   113

114

pivoted 90 degrees to the left to gain momentum for the counter-attack.

113. Immediately the larger fighter grabs the attacking arm and pivots back 90 degrees and kicks to the knee. It is important for the pull to be powerful and coordinated with the momentum-giving pivot. If the opponent's balance is not destroyed, he may attack to the side of the larger fighter's body, which is exposed by the *bong sao*. This ends the attack.

114. Against the larger fighter's straight punch, a *taun sao* is used in defense and an offensive kick to the testicles delivered.

115   116   117

118   119

115. This is followed up by a stomping knee-kick.

116. The same stomping knee-kick could also be delivered on the other side.

117. The stomping knee-kick could also be combined with a *taun sao* and punch.

118. Then the larger fighter can be attacked with the cross-body cutting palm-strike.

119. Finally, against a straight punch, this throwing technique from the wooden-dummy form may be used. The larger fighter's foot is locked up as shown and he is thrown backwards by the execution of both a foot and hand technique.

120

120. Here the throw occurs. The hand technique is more than a push—it is a jolting drive right through the chest. The foot which lifts the opponent's leg should not leave the ground, but drives backwards as if kicking with the calf muscle.

2

The Wing Chun Butterfly Knives

CLASSICAL WEAPONS IN THE AGE OF THE GUN

There are various schools of thought about training with classical weapons such as the Wing Chun butterfly knives and the six-and-a-half pole; (*see* J.E. Mayberry, "The Great Weapons Debate: To Train or Not to Train?" *Black Belt* 22[2]: 72-76, 92-93 [February 1984]).

Many modern practitioners of the martial arts see classical weapons as dated in the age of the gun, bomb, and laser beam. The butterfly knives cannot be easily carried, and the six-and-a-half pole is too long (7 feet 2 inches) to be passed off as a walking stick! Moreover, there can be little doubt that at any range, even an air rifle (especially a repeater) is a superior weapon to a stick or blade. However, in defense of the classical position on the contemporary relevance of blade and stick weapons, the following points can be made:

(1) Some situations, especially in the apprehending of unarmed suspects in police work, may arise where the use of a firearm is unjustified, but it is too dangerous to rely upon unarmed combat skills.

(2) You may not have a gun at the time of attack, or you may lose your gun or run out of bullets. You may be forced to rely upon secondary weapons that have to be found in the environment or improvised.

Other martial-arts experts are critical of weapons training because it places too great a reliance upon the weapon. In this philosophy, the belief is sometimes expressed that the hand or foot is the only weapon needed. However, nice as this sounds, this belief is a myth. An armed and skilled fighter will clearly defeat an unarmed skilled fighter, unless the armed fighter makes a stupid mistake. The unarmed fighter in this situation cannot afford to make any mistakes. An armed, unskilled, but intelligent fighter (depending upon the weapon used), is quite capable of defeating the average unarmed martial artist. Pitting an armed, unskilled, intelligent fighter against an unarmed, expert martial artist is a contest which will depend upon the kind of weapon employed—a repeating firearm offering near hopeless odds, and a blade-weapon somewhat better odds. The slaughter of great Chinese martial artists in the Boxer Rebellion of 1900, by relatively poorly trained foreign troops with rifles, demonstrates the falsity of the hand is my sword philosophy. Weapons training should supplement unarmed training, not replace it. Weapons (including firearms and especially handguns) should be extensions of the body and the fighter should be sufficiently flexible to be able to see the relevance of his classical weapons training in the real world. The spirit behind the use of the Wing Chun weapons is quite consistent with this pragmatic attitude.

THE NATURE OF WING CHUN BUTTERFLY KNIVES

The Wing Chun butterfly knives *(bart jarm dao)* were said to have originally been carried by the monks of the Sil Lum Temple in their travels. They were typically hidden in the monks' long boots, and were designed for close-range fighting with a knife in each hand. The knife is equal in length to the practitioner's fist and forearm. If the knife is too short, then it offers less protection when it is rotated onto the forearm as a block or for an elbow smash or slash. If the knife is too long, then safe rotation inside the arms is not possible.

A satisfactory Wing Chun butterfly knife is identified by the shape of the "ear" of the knife. The ear is used not only to lock up and trap weapons (analogous to the traps of *chi sao*); it is also used for rotating the weapon, similar to the use of the *sai* in karate. As the butterfly knife has only one sharp edge, the blunt top edge of the knife can be aligned along the forearm for blocking or for elbow smashes or slashes. The knives can also be rotated so that they are aligned together (handle to handle) to create a longer blocking area (the number one knife skill or *yut ge dao*). I shall discuss all of this in more detail later. The important point to note here is that the ear of a satisfactory Wing Chun butterfly knife is curved like a *sai*; it is not flat. You cannot satisfactorily rotate a flat ear because it catches on your thumb.

The butterfly knives also involve many close-to-the-body hand moves. These moves are similar to some of the moves found in the *Sil Lum Tao* form. The *gaun dao* and *taun dao* in section four of the butterfly-knives form are close-to-the-body movements, designed to deflect an attack over the widest possible area, which is consistent with the philosophy of close-range combat. However, under no circumstances are butterfly knives rotated so that the point of the blade faces the chest—for obvious reasons. This move is not part of any sane knife skill.

The butterfly-knives form is not derived from the *Chum Kil* form, but is based upon the *Bil Jee* form. In fact, it is said that the *Bil Jee* form was added as a type of preliminary training for the butterfly-knives form. There is only one skill in the *Chum Kil* form that even vaguely resembles a knife skill (the *gaun sao*), while the *Bil Jee* form certainly looks like it could be performed with knives, the darting fingers being replaced by blades. It goes almost without saying that there are no jumping or spinning techniques in the Wing Chun butterfly-knives form as I conceive it, because there are no jumping or spinning techniques in the Wing Chun system that I study. You do not, if you can help it, turn your back on an opponent—especially one with a weapon.

ANALYSIS OF THE BUTTERFLY-KNIVES FORM

The stance used in performing the butterfly-knives form is the small circle triangular footwork, a stance similar to the Wing Chun fighting stance, only the distance between the knees is slightly greater as the fighter stands more upright with less bending of the knees. The center of gravity of the body is therefore higher, for relatively fast movements. Walking involves stepping forward with the back foot, whilst maintaining the Wing Chun stance—this differs from the forward-foot-first shuffling footwork used in very close-range fighting. While the wide horse-stance is used for balance in the six-and-a-half pole form, it is not generally used in the butterfly-knives form. The exception to this is in the second section of the knives form, where in thrusting the blade the practitioner sometimes sinks into a wide horse-stance and pivots to put his body weight behind the thrusts. But this is the exception, not the rule.

The butterfly-knives form has eight sections, and each section has one important skill that I will now summarize. The actual form is complex and impossible to summarize concisely verbally, so I shall allow the photographs to speak for themselves.

Section One. This section introduces the basic chopping motion, or *darm dao.* The chops are directed through a plane passing through the median axis of the fighter's body which offers the shortest distance between the knife blade and the object of attack.

After completing the set of four chops, beginning first with the left hand and then with the right, there is a downward jolt of both knives, blades perpendicular to the ground, similar to the downward palm-strike or *gaum sao* in the close of the *Chum Kil* form. This move is known as the *gaum dao,* and in the opening of each section it separates the performance of the central technique into two sequences, the first beginning on the left-hand side and the second beginning on the right-hand side. Section one also features a double thrusting action of the knives, designed to lock up a thrusting weapon. The outer knife then curves around the weapon in the *haun dao* move (analogous to the opening movement of *haun sao* in the *Sil Lum Tao*), and a chop is delivered with the other knife.

Section Two. This section introduces the *doy dao,* or thrust. The practitioner moves forward performing a high to low defense *(gaun dao)* and a chop *(jarm dao).* As the opponent moves backward to the starting point, he performs a side *gaum dao* and thrust, as in section one. Sometimes after the thrust, a rotation of the weapon is performed with a chop following. In combat, this rotation is used to get around a guard and to attack with a *jarm dao.*

Section Three. The basic skill here is the combination of a *taun dao* and a *jarm dao,* or to deflect or *taun* a weapon away and to chop through the opening. The use of this skill is analogous to the *taun sao* and chop practiced in the *Sil Lum Tao.*

Section Four. In this section, the basic skill practiced is the combination of a *gaun dao* (low defense) and a *taun dao,* a skill that was already practiced in the *Bil Jee* form. However, what is frequently omitted from this section is the close-to-the-body movements of the knives. The *taun dao* in this section resembles the internal *taun sao* from the *Sil Lum Tao.* As I have said, this technique has been especially designed for close-range defense.

Section Five. Here we see the often misunderstood, combined technique of the *kuaun dao,* or *taun dao/bong dao.* I say misunderstood, because it is sometimes thought by students that the low *bong dao* can be used as a block. However, a knife held in this fashion is not a strong block. Rather, the *bong dao* is a surprise attack. The opponent's attack is met by a defensive *taun dao,* the weapon is *tauned* or moved out, and the knife held in the *bong dao* hand formation cuts the opponent from the groin up. The spirit of this under-the-bridge (from a low position to strike under a guard) attack comes from the *Bil Jee* form.

Section Six. The number one knife skill (*yut ge dao)* has already been mentioned. The point of this move is to create a larger blocking area. In the form, the fighter moves forward performing the number one knife defense. Then the top knife is spun onto the forearm for a solid defense. The lower knife is rotated into the normal grip, as the fighter walks forward and performs an underhand cut from the groin up of the (imaginary) opponent. This is yet another example of the use of the under-the-bridge, or below-the-guard attack from the *Bil Jee* form. No truly satisfactory butterfly-knives form can neglect these deceptive methods of attack.

Section Seven. The *man dao,* or side asking-blade, is another skill that can be recognized in the *Bil Jee* form. It is used as a side defense with the blade swung from low-to-high, again to cover a large area. It can also be used as an attack in the fashion already described in sections five and six.

Section Eight. This section features the combination of a *gaun dao* (low defense) and a *gway dao* (elbow smash). In addition, it also features a powerful technique—the pivot and chop. Its obvious use is to deliver a powerful chop with the body weight behind it to an opponent attacking you from the rear. In this form, we also see, as in section six, the use of the *par dao* or parry knife, and chop. This technique is used to deflect an attack as in its unarmed analogue, the deflection being with the flat of the blade. In fighting, a strike with the flat of the blade can be delivered to an opponent to prevent a fatal injury. However, as in all other cases of knife fighting, use of these weapons typically leads to serious, if not fatal injuries. The reader should keep in mind that these weapons are not toys and that if any of these techniques are used, then legal and moral consequences must be faced.

It is also worth noting that the butterfly-knives form clarifies another misconception about Wing Chun kung-fu—that there is no backward footwork and that a fighter never retreats. Any good general knows when to retreat and so does any sane fighter. Some Wing Chun fighters also retreat when the going gets too tough. In any case the thesis that there is no backward footwork in Wing Chun is contradicted by the backward step in the *Chum Kil* form. Backward steps are also seen in all sections of the butterfly-knives form

I have said that the Wing Chun butterfly-knife skills are still relevant to modern self-defense. Once the principles governing the use of these weapons have been grasped, you may look for suitable analogues in your environment in a desperate self-defense situation. Two sticks, two short iron bars, or two bottles whose bottoms you can break off are some examples. Street punks have always used these sorts of weapons in desperate situations. I do not recommend that you do this yourself, unless your life is at stake—but, on the other hand, you must be prepared for the unexpected.

It is not usually recognized that Wing Chun kung-fu has throwing weapons. The weapons used are not as spectacular as the *shuriken* used in the Japanese ninja arts, but they are often more practical; thus, the Wing Chun skills may therefore be of more use today where it is regarded as an offense in many cities to even carry sharpened *shuriken*. Coins can be used as *shuriken,* and they need not be sharpened to be effective. Small stones or chopsticks, darts, and even ball-point pens can also be thrown. These weapons may be hidden in the clothing as secret support weapons or used as distraction weapons. The throwing weapons were added to the Wing Chun system by Fung Ching, a high-ranking policeman, during the Ching dynasty.

Wing Chun weapons are thrown from the center-line of the body, usually using the *fook sao* hand shape for concealment when using them in diversionary fighting tactics. Weapons are not thrown in the hand-raised-above-the-head fashion of modern knife throwing. The whipping overhead throw (commonly used to throw hand grenades) is also not used. Instead, a whipping underhand throw which resembles the *til sao* movement is employed. Another useful throw employs the force of a *jut sao* to project the coin or stone through the center-line. The side asking-hand is also used in throwing.

All of these throws are based upon basic Wing Chun hand moves especially designed for close-range throwing; close range being defined as the effective fighting range of the six-and-a-half pole. A Wing Chun fighter armed with only the butterfly knives would have difficulty fighting against an opponent armed with a spear or a six-and-a-half pole. A strike with a throwing weapon against such a foe may enable the knifeman to safely bridge the gap and put his opponent out of commission. In desperate situations (such as a long weapon in a skilled hand, against which one cannot bridge the gap), one butterfly knife might be thrown at a foe, the other being used to kill him immediately after the strike. Because of the size of the blade, the knife is thrown as one would throw an axe with the usual target being the opponent's chest to maximize the probability of a strike. It is unusual, of course, to use a short sword in this way, but with training it can be done.

Finally, a comment on politics. No doubt my Wing Chun knife form, and indeed any of the skills discussed in my books may differ from those of another master. No student of mine is ever allowed to say that another master is no good or his skill is not authentic. The martial arts are dynamic and evolutionary arts that allow room for individual differences in interpretation, and in a free society these differences must be respected. I therefore have no interest whatsoever in political issues such as who is a real master and what is authentic Wing Chun; I have no desire to offend anyone involved in the martial arts whatsoever. I offer you material for thought: take what you find to be true and useful and discard the rest with an attitude of humble respect for different opinions. That, after all, is what scientific thinkers—and great men like Bruce Lee—have always done.

121   122   123

THE WING CHUN BUTTERFLY KNIVES

Note: to avoid needless and confusing repetition of sequenced photographs, some photographs of movements which are constantly repeated are deleted after their initial appearance, and a reference note made. Students should refer to the glossary for a definition of terms used in the following instructions.

SECTION ONE

121. Stand in the basic attention position, the back and legs straight, right arm by the side, cradling both knives in left arm.

122. Punch with the right hand.

123. Begin cross-hand move (the turning of the wrist in various directions with fingers up and rigid).

124 125 126

127 128 129

124. Wrist turn to the left.
125. Wrist turn down.
126. Wrist turn to the right.
127. Close fist.
128. Withdraw fist. Return to attention position as described previously.
129. Bend knees.
130. Turn knees out.

130   131   132

133   134   135

131. Turn heels in to form the parallel stance.

132. Left foot moves forward, right hand touches knives.

133. Deliver a right foot heel-kick.

134. Perform *gaum dao* (double downward knife-block).

135. Begin the chopping technique—four chops follow—left, right, left, right. Then repeat *gaum dao*. The chops are delivered with power—imagine cutting an opponent's skull in two.

136   137   138

136. Now deliver another four chops—right, left, right, left. Then repeat *gaum dao*.

137. Then step forward with weapon-locking technique. (An opponent's weapon would be locked between the two knives, pinned between the blades. This enables a more stable trap to be executed by using the ear of one of the blades, whilst striking with the other. This technique can be used against any rigid striking weapon, such as a sword or stick.)

138. Now use *haun dao* to move the (imaginary) weapon out of the center-line and down, then chop with the other blade. The *haun dao* is a rotating knife move, used with circular wrist actions to move a weapon which is locked up, in a particular direction, so that a strike can be secured. (These rotating knife moves are exactly analogous to the empty-hand *haun sao* seen in volume one.)

139. Move backwards to start position, performing side *gaum dao* three times alternating right . . .

140. . . . then left and finally right again. Then execute a front *gaum dao* as shown previously.

Repeat this sequence on the opposite side to complete this section of the form, reversing the respective moves for the left and right hands; that which was done first on the left, is now done on the right and so on. Conclude with *gaum dao*.

139   140

141   142   143

SECTION TWO

141. Perform four thrusts with the knives—left, right, left, right—and then *gaum dao.*

142. Then perform another four thrusts with the knives—right, left, right, left—and then *gaum dao.*

143. Move forward three steps performing *gaun dao* (low defense) and chop.

144   145   146

144. Repeat the *gaun dao* and chop three times. Move backwards as in section one, simply reversing the steps that took you forward, whilst performing the side *gaum dao* (a high-to-low downward chop of the blade, used to defend the lower body).

Repeat this sequence on the opposite side, reversing the respective moves for the left and right hands. Conclude with *gaum dao*.

SECTION THREE

145. Perform the *taun dao* (analogous to the *taun sao*, a deflective parry with the blunt edge of the blade), and chop—whilst pivoting—left, right, left, right. Then do a *gaum dao*.

146. Repeat the *taun dao* and chop sequence, this time pivoting—right, left, right, left. Again do a *gaum dao*.

Move forward three steps as in section two (left, right, left,) performing *gaun dao* and chop (left chop, right *gaun dao;* right chop, left *gaun dao;* left chop right *gaun dao*).

147. Now move backwards to start position, deliver a left chop.

148. Follow this by a right chop.

149. Then do another left chop, followed by *gaum dao*.

Repeat this sequence on the opposite side reversing the respective moves for the left and right hands. Conclude with *gaum dao*.

147   148   149

150   151   152

SECTION FOUR

150. Now perform *gaun dao* (low defense) and *taun dao*, pivoting—left, right, left, right, changing the hand position with each change in direction. Begin with left *gaun dao* and right *taun dao*. Conclude with *gaum dao*, pivoting back to the front position.

151. Again repeat *gaun dao* (low defense) and *taun dao*, pivoting—right, left, right, left. Conclude with *gaum dao*, pivoting back to the front position.

152. Move forward, *taun dao* with the left, and chop with the right.

153	154	155

153. *Taun dao* with right and chop with left.

154. Finally, *taun dao* with left and chop on the right.

155. Retreat three steps back to start position, with three chops as in previous section; in the sequence, step-chop, step-chop, the forward foot moving backwards first. Perform *gaum dao*.

Now repeat this sequence on the opposite side reversing the respective moves for the left and right hands. Conclude with *gaum dao*.

SECTION FIVE

156. Perform *taun dao* and *bong dao* (i.e. analogous to the *bong sao*), pivoting 180 degrees to the left with left *taun dao* and right *bong dao*, reversing hand techniques with each 180-degree pivot.

157. Pivot to the right 180 degrees, perform *taun dao* and *bong dao*. Then pivot to the left 180 degrees and right 180 degrees again, both times performing these moves.

158. Move forward with the *taun dao/bong dao* formation as shown.

159. Now strike under the bridge with the knife that was in the *bong dao*.

Conclude this section of the form with the three chops whilst walking backwards three steps to the start position, as done previously. Perform *gaum dao*.

Then repeat this sequence on the opposite side reversing the respective moves for the left and right hands.

156   157   158

159   160   161

SECTION SIX

160. Now form the number one knife or *yut ge dao* (i.e. the knives are held to offer maximum defensive protection), rotating the knives using the ear of the knives, first to the left . . .

161. . . . then to the right. Repeat again to the left, and then to the right.

162   163   164

165   166

162. Now step forward with the knives held in the number one knife position.

163. Then cut from low to high (i.e. under the bridge) with the knife.

164. Immediately form a double block (a guard against a sword smash), with the left hand in normal position, the right hand in reverse grip, with the right knife's blunt edge aligned along the forearm for a powerful defense.

165. From this, parry with the left knife, chop with the right.

166. Conclude as seen previously with the three chops whilst walking backwards.

Repeat this sequence on the opposite side, reversing the respective moves for the left and right hands. Conclude with *gaum dao*.

SECTION SEVEN

167. Perform the side asking-knife, a low-to-high sweep with the blade, to the left. The fighter's stance now changes to the parallel stance for stability whilst executing this technique. Further, the aim of the side asking-knife is to defend the body with a low-to-high sweep and it would be a mistake then to offer a wider area of attack on the side to the opponent.

168. Then perform the side asking-knife to the right. Repeat to the left and to the right again.

169. Now walk forward with a left side asking-knife cutting from low to high.

170

171

172

173

170. Then parry and chop. Retreat whilst chopping as done previously.

Repeat this sequence on the opposite side reversing the respective moves for the left and right hands. Conclude with *gaum dao*.

SECTION EIGHT

171. Perform a *gaum dao* (low defense) and *gway dao* (elbow smash) to the left.

172. Then pivot 180 degrees to the right and repeat the *gaum dao*

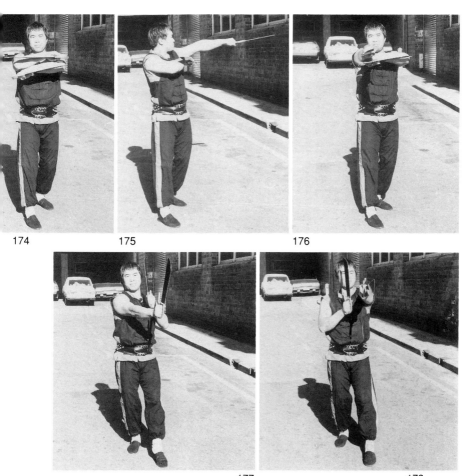

174   175   176

177   178

and *gway dao*. Then pivot to the left and right again, repeating this move each time.

173. Now walk forward, with a *gaun dao* and chop.

174. Then form the double bar-knife. This can be used as a defense, but it is primarily an intermediate technique or position, in preparation for a side chop.

175. Pivot 90 degrees to the left and chop from under the bridge. Repeat to the right, left, and then right. Return to the position shown in Figure 174.

176. Facing front-on, chop from under the bridge.

177. Then take a step and parry and chop.

178. Now retreat backwards three steps to the start position, whilst chopping three times as seen previously. Perform *gaum dao*.

179

180

181

Repeat this sequence on the opposite side reversing the respective moves for the left and right hands. Conclude with *gaum dao*.

179. In parallel stance, cross blades together, and moving in a circular fashion, scrape the blades together as if exposing their sharpness to an opponent.

180. Conclude this movement with the blades by your side, in a parallel stance.

181. Heels in, toes in, knees straight, stand at attention (as in Figure 121) to conclude the form.

3

The Six-and-a-Half Pole Form

THE POINT OF POLE TRAINING

The six-and-a-half pole, so named not because of its length (which is actually 7 feet 2 inches), but because of the number of techniques in the form, was not an original part of the Wing Chun system. The knowledge that came to form the Wing Chun pole form came from a Buddhist monk named Shin Chi, who was originally a monk in the Sil Lum Temple, well-known for his martial-arts skills. It is said that he fled the Sil Lum Temple and took refuge upon the famous Red Junk. There, Shin taught pole techniques for combat to Leung Yee Tai, a poler on this boat, using a shorter pole that was 7 feet 2 inches long and tapered to a point (like a cue stick). This pole was known as a rat's tail stick and was both strong and flexible. Wong Wah Bo was a Chinese-opera singer and an excellent Wing Chun fighter who once travelled on this boat. He traded knowledge with Wing Chun master Leung Yee Tai and the pole form was added to Wing Chun. Leung Yee Tai later taught Leung Jan, who in turn taught Leung Bic and Wah Shun.

The Wing Chun pole techniques are still of relevance in modern combat. Of course, nobody today fights with a pole, spear, or lance. Indeed, the last recorded use of the lance by the British was in the Boer War (*see* D. Featherstone, "The Lance," in *Weapons and Equipment of the Victorian Soldier* [Poole, Dorset: Blandford Press, 1978], pp. 53-57). However the bayonet, a blade attached to the muzzle of a rifle, is a weapon still used by the military. Typically, bayonets are fixed when ammunition is expended and hand-to-hand fighting is to be engaged in. An expert in the six-and-a-half pole would also be an expert in bayonet fighting. I have examined a number of military manuals with chapters on bayonet fighting and have found that the fighting skills are virtually identical. There would be much less of a transfer if the student studied some other classical weapons form such as the Chinese broad sword or saber (although I have heard of a Hsing-i pole form that was adapted for the bayonet).

The long pole is also used in the Wing Chun system as a weight-training tool, serving as a leverage bar. The pole can be used as a weight-training device for the whole musculature of the arms, especially the forearms. The student may experiment with one-arm lifts, and if particularly strong, steel pipes or solid steel rods may be used. Weight plates may also be placed upon the end of the pole. This method of weight training, using a leverage bar, was apparently used by many old-time Western strongmen, but today with expensive modern equipment these inexpensive training methods are sadly being forgotten. If the reader cannot afford to join a health club or gym, then pole training is a good way to develop upper-body strength.

ANALYSIS OF THE SIX-AND-A-HALF POLE FORM

The six-and-a-half pole form is probably the simplest martial-arts weapon form. It can be summarized in only one paragraph. The practitioner stands in a wide horse-stance (because of its low center of gravity) to supply a power base, holding the pole as one holds a barbell in performing the deadlift—the hand closest to the end of the pole is in a palm-down grip, while the other hand is in a palm-up grip. The pole is gripped close to one end, not in the middle as some staff fighters grip their sticks. This is to maximize the distance between you and your opponent. In addition, the pole is also used as a lever—in striking to the side or up or down, the hands move in circular arcs. The action is the same as if you were using a crow bar to lift a rock. The form, in all its beautiful simplicity is as follows:

1. Thrust, or *chir gwon.* The thrust has a drilling, spiral action to it for penetration.

2. *Til gwon.* This is similar to the *til sao* action in the *Sil Lum Tao.* It is used to either lift a weapon or to strike an opponent from the groin up. Remember that the pole is tapered, and is strong and flexible. Used with inch-force, it has an impulse like a whip. The *til gwon* is performed in the hanging stance, or *dil mah* stance. The back foot remains flat on the ground. The lead foot however is lifted, the heel remaining off the ground, the toes lightly touching the floor so that you remain ready to transfer your body weight forward in attack.

3. Left-side parry.

4. Right-side parry.

5. *Jut gwon,* or the downward snap of the stick to strike from the head down.

6. *Til gwon* up again to strike to the groin.

The form concludes with the outward push of the stick, said to be a half technique.

The important thing to learn about Wing Chun pole fighting is *chi gwon,* or the sticky-stick techniques. As in sticky-hands, the principle here is to cling with your stick to the opponent's weapon and to clear an entrance for a strike. This is done by *til gwon, jut gwon,* or the left- or right-side parry. It is also a favorite trick of pole fighters to slide their pole down the opponent's weapon (if it has no guard) and attack the fingers, or alternatively to attack the hands and arms with the *til gwon* or *jut gwon.* In many cases, with the proper rat's tail stick, the tapered end is so fast and flexible that it whips around a guard. For this reason, Wing Chun practitioners tend to train with non-tapered sticks, even if protective gear is worn.

Sticky-sticks can however, be practiced with a partner using thin plastic pipes with the appropriate protective gear. It is also useful to practice thrusting at a target to develop accuracy. It is ideal, with all due respect to Mother Nature, to go out into the bush or the wilds with a pole, and practice thrusts, lifts, and parries on the branches of trees.

Beyond these remarks, there are no further secret techniques to master in the use of the Wing Chun pole. Once the student has internalized the idea of *chi gwon,* training must be geared toward developing strength, speed, and flexibility in the use of the pole. This training will feedback into unarmed fighting skills, further develop-ing your martial-art physique.

In the introduction to this book, I said that the Wing Chun

weapons are still relevant today as weapons in themselves. Earlier in this chapter I mentioned the relevance of the six-and-a-half pole techniques to bayonet fighting. However, the six-and-a-half pole is worth learning for self-defense in daily life when either you have no gun, or you prefer not to use it. Once the basic principle of chi gwon is grasped and the six-and-a-half techniques thoroughly mastered, any number of environmental objects could serve as a make-do pole. These include pieces of steel rod from a building site, stakes used to hold up small trees in the park, pieces of scrap wood and scrap pipe or iron grill, and various tools such as brooms, rakes, shovels, and so on. Indeed, the humble umbrella, especially if it has a metal point, can be a devastating weapon in the hand of a trained pole fighter. For that reason, then, I believe that the Wing Chun six-and-a-half pole is still relevant to self-defense in modern society.

182   183

184

THE SIX-AND-A-HALF POLE FORM

182.   Begin the form in a natural walking stance, feet approximately shoulder-width distance apart. The pole is held low and to the left. The left hand grips such that the palm faces away from the body; the right hand grips such that the palm faces the body.

183.   Curl the pole up (as if curling a bar bell), then take a step forward with the left foot and thrust the pole out perpendicular to your center-line, to the full extension of your arms.

184. Then move the pole back to your chest, and sink into the wide horse-stance of karate, feet roughly twice the width of your hips, the knees bent at a 90-degree angle, the back straight. The center of gravity is thus much lower than it would be in the normal walking stance.

185   186

187   188

185. The thrust to the left (*chir gwon*) is performed with a drilling or screwing motion of the arms for maximum penetration.

186. Now raise the pole up (*til gwon*) changing to the *dil mah* or hanging stance (similar to the cat stance of karate) The stance is reached by retreating into it.

187. Move the pole in a parry to the left (high section).

188. Then parry with the pole to the right (high section).

189

190

189. Now suddenly snap the pole downwards (*jut gwon*) attacking the opponent from high-to-low.

190. Then perform *til gwon*, as seen previously, to strike up to the groin.

Conclude the form by returning to the position shown in Figure 182.

191   192

193   194

COMBAT APPLICATIONS OF THE WING CHUN
WEAPONS

191. The knifeman and the poleman square off.

192. Against the straight thrust of the pole, the knifeman locks up the pole with the locking knife action from section one of the butterfly-knives form.

193. The knifeman then leaps forward, simultaneously sliding the knife along the pole to cut the fingers of the poleman.

194. Finally, a chop to the forehead is delivered.

195. The poleman makes a powerful *jut gwon* or downward attack with the pole. This is stopped with the double knife-block from section six of the form.

196. The knifeman moves in closer performing *gaun dao* (low defense) to control the pole and chopping to the forehead.

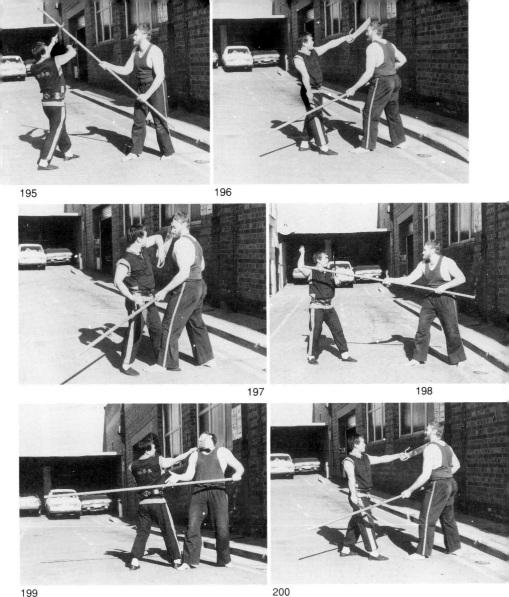

195

196

197

198

199

200

197. This is then followed up by an elbow smash with the blade to the face.

198. A side strike with the pole is delivered which is blocked by a parry.

199. The knifeman then slides his knives down the pole, and suddenly turns 180 degrees, slashing the poleman across the throat.

200. Then the pole is locked up and controlled with the right *gaun dao* whilst a powerful knife thrust to the throat is made.

201   202

203   204

201. Against the same type of downward strike, a chopping parry is made, opening up the poleman's center-line.

202. A chop is made through this opening to the head.

203. The same downward attack can also be defended against by the side asking-knife.

204. The knifeman faces the swordsman who is about to deliver a powerful overhead smash with a sword.

205. The knifeman moves to the (right) side, parries the sword and chops to the temple.

206. Alternatively the knifeman could have moved to the left, parried the attack and also chopped to the head.

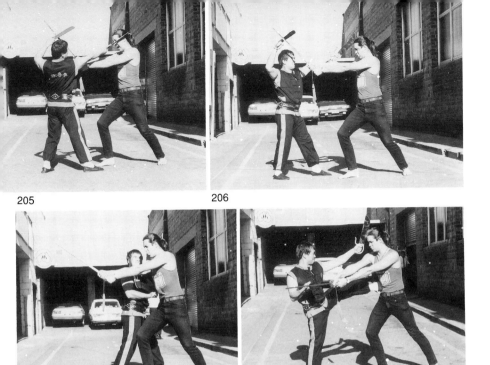

205
206

207
208

209

207. The knifeman then moves in closer and slices to the chest.

208. Kicking attacks can be used simultaneously with blade fights, especially when weapons are locked up. Here the swordsman's weapon is blocked and a chop to the head and kick to the mid-section is delivered, perhaps as something of an overkill.

209. Here the swordsman's weapon is blocked and a kick to the knee and simultaneous chop to the throat delivered.

Conclusion

This concludes my guide to the Wing Chun system. I have outlined all of its forms—*Sil Lum Tao, Chum Kil,* and *Bil Jee,* as well as its fighting skills and weapons sets. I have not put into these books every single technique I know, but have rather strived for generality, attempting to isolate the basic principles of combat behind the art. I hope my approach has been a truly scientific and analytical one, sensitive to both the merits and limits of Wing Chun kung-fu. Sadly, this approach is seldom adopted in the martial arts; although it must be adopted if they are to gain intellectual respectability, making them a subject for serious intellectual investigation in the West.

Wing Chun kung-fu is a dynamic, evolutionary art. Masters have constantly modified and added to it. For example, in the early days fighters apparently fought in the little horse-stance. The addition of sticky-leg skills meant that this wide stance had to be eliminated. Likewise in the second book in this series I also suggested modifications to classical Wing Chun, adding the long arm circular-fist of White Crane kung-fu, Western boxing hand techniques, and the *Muay Thai* elbow strikes, knee kicks, and footwork. I argued that all of the above can be added without compromising classical Wing Chun and that all of these elements can form a functional, systematically harmonious whole, rather than a non-classical mess. I believe it is possible to completely evade Bruce Lee's great problem of classical versus non-classical systems. This is done by operating with a plurality of styles that complement each other, supplying missing skills that the other system lacks. The systems are unified by a common meta-philosophy of combat, along with physical principles of biomechanics and universal scientific principles of reason.

I hope that these guidebooks serve to eliminate the many confusions concerning the Wing Chun system, and that both my own presentation, and suggestions for change will serve to enrich Wing Chun kung-fu. Moreover, I hope that the approach adopted in these volumes founded upon critical scientific reason, will be of interest to students of other martial arts, both traditional and non-traditional.

Glossary

Bart Jarm Dao The Wing Chun butterfly knives. The length of these double knives is the same distance as between the little knuckle on the fighter's clenched fist to the point of the elbow, to enable the entire forearm to be covered by a blade in blocking.

basic attention-position The fighter stands upright with his back straight, eyes focused straight ahead upon the horizon, feet together and hands by the sides.

bil jee One of the most useful hand strikes in Wing Chun, it is featured in the set form of the same name (*see next entry*).

Bil Jee The thrusting-fingers form, which was traditionally taught only to the most trusted students.

bong dao The *bong dao* is analogous to the *bong sao*. The arm is held in the *bong sao* formation at chest level with the knife held so that the entire length of the blade faces the opponent and the point of the blade points to the ground. This knife move is not used as a block, rather it is a surprise attack. As the opponent's attack is met by a defensive *taun dao*, the weapon is *tauned* or moved out, and the knife held in the *bong dao* hand formation cuts the opponent from the groin up.

bong sao One of the most important hand movements in Wing Chun; a bent-elbow hand formation, such that the blade of the hand faces upward.

center-line theory The center-line is an imaginary line that passes through the median axis of the body where the most vulnerable organs are located. The center-line theory therefore requires that the fighter should defend this area by keeping his elbows in the center-line in both defense and attack, while attempting to penetrate to the center-line of the opponent.

chi (Pek: *ch'i, qi*) Actually meaning breath, *chi* is used to describe the intrinsic psycho-physical energy used in the internal arts.

chi gerk Wing Chun's sticky-leg attacks.

chi gwon Also known as sticky-sticks, analogous to *chi sao*. The principle is to cling with the stick to the opponent's weapon and clear an entrance for a strike.

Chi Kung (Pek: *ch'i kung, qigong*) A type of training to obtain an inner harmony of the body and spirit. It is becoming well known in the West as a method to develop one's internal psychic energy.

chil ying The name of the well-known, front-facing fighting position, in which the fighter stands in parallel stance (*kim nur mar*).

chin-na The grappling moves of Wing Chun.

chir gwon A drilling spiral thrust with the six-and-a-half pole.

chi sao The Wing Chun sticky-hand techniques.

Chum Kil The bridging the gap form of Wing Chun, which introduces three kicks into the Wing Chun system.

darm dao A basic butterfly-knives chopping attack wherein chops are directed through a plane passing through the median axis of the fighter's body.

dil mah Also known as the hanging stance in the six-and-a-half pole form. The back foot remains flat on the ground, the lead foot however is lifted, the heel remaining off the ground, the toes lightly touching the floor, so that the body weight is ready to be transferred forward in an attack.

ding An upward-lifting wrist movement used in Wing Chun, not so much as a block but to open up an opponent's guard.

dit dat jow A herbal medicine whose name means warm-strike-wine, which is used to prevent arthritis, to heal bruises, to toughen the skin of striking surfaces, and to relieve the pain that results either from over-training or from sustaining a contact injury.

doy dao A thrust with the butterfly knife, analogous to the *bil jee* finger thrust. The continuous thrusting action of both knives involves under-the-bridge strikes (strikes moving from from low-to-high, to penetrate under a guard). Viewed side-on from the left, the blades move in a clockwise curvilinear path, so that the hands are never beneath a sharp blade.

fook sao The hooking, lying-on-top hand typically used to redirect attacks.

Futshan Pai A Wing Chun association located in mainland China, in Futshan, where Wing Chun was originated in the eighteenth century by a nun and herbal physician named Ng Mui. The name is now also used to describe the style taught in Futshan.

gaum dao   A downward jolt of both butterfly knives, blades perpendicular to the ground, similar to the downward palm-strike *gaum sao* in the close of the *Chum Kil* form. In the opening of each section of the butterfly-knives form it separates the performance of the central technique into two sequences, the first beginning on the left-hand side and the second beginning on the right-hand side.

gaun dao A downward chop with the butterfly knife, analogous to the *gaun sao,* designed to offer a high-to-low sweeping defense to protect the upper body.

gaun sao   A downward chopping defense that completely protects the upper body.

ging (ching) Inch-force; an immense inner power that can be utilized against an opponent at close range for an explosive shock-wave effect.

guard position The lead defensive arm is extended in the center-line so that the angle between the biceps and the forearm is about 150 degrees, with the hand held in the *wu sao* position. The rear defensive hand is also held in the *wu sao* position, at a distance of about a fist-and-a-half from the chest.

gum sao A Wing Chun push-down block that pushes an opponent's kick away from the body, using the palm of the hand.

gway dao An elbow-smash with the butterfly knife. The knife is spun so that the blunt edge of the blade rests along the forearm in shield-like fashion and the blade can be slashed along an opponent from high-to-low and low-to-high, and from inside and outside the guard.

haun dao A technique analogous to the opening-up movement of *haun sao* in the *Sil Lum Tao,* using the butterfly knife to rotate around a weapon by rotating the wrist, and hence to secure a strike, either with that knife, or else to move the opponent's weapon away, creating an opening to strike with the other weapon.

haun sao A wrist-rotating movement, used to twist around guards, or to open up a guard.

jarm dao The basic chopping action of the Wing Chun butterfly knives. (*See Bart Jarm Dow.*)

jut sao A sudden downward jerk with the edge of the heel of the hand, to clear a pathway for a strike.

jut gwon A downward snap of the six-and-a-half pole, to strike from the head down.

kim nur mar The Wing Chun parallel stance, in which the fighter stands such that both knees and toes point inward toward the median axis of the body.

kuaun dao The combined technique of *taun dao* with one hand and a *bong dao* with the other. See *bong dao.*

kung Extraordinary intrinsic force that can be tapped into and used after proper development through years of intense kung-fu (*chi kung*) training.

kung-fu Originally a Chinese term that meant simply an intense concentration of energy. Later, through popularization of the styles, it came to be synonymous with Chinese martial arts, especially those of the Shaolin lineage.

la The drawing-down hand of Wing Chun.

man dao The side asking-knife is a defense with the blade from low-to-high to cover a large area. It can also be used as an attack, slashing from the groin up.

Muay Thai Thai kick-boxing.

pak sao A defensive parry.

parallel stance *see kim nur mar*

par dao Here the knife is used to parry a weapon, and as in its unarmed analogue, this technique is used to deflect an attack, the deflection being with the flat of the blade.

Sil Lum Tao The first form of the Wing Chun system, the name means the Way of the Small Thought. (It is sometimes seen written as *Shil Lim Tao*.)

six-and-a-half pole The Wing Chun long pole (7 feet 2 inches) was introduced into the system by a Buddhist monk named Shin Chi, who fled from the destruction of the Sil Lum Temple and took refuge upon the famous Red Junk, where he taught his pole techniques to Leung Yee Tai. They used a 7-foot-2-inch pole tapered to a point, known as a rat's tail stick. The expression six-and-a-half refers to the number of techniques in the form.

small circle triangular footwork Wing Chun footwork is small circle, meaning that it is especially designed for close-range fighting where balance is extremely important. The footwork is said to be triangular because a line drawn through the median axis of both the rear and lead feet would form a triangle.

som kwok bo The correct fighting stance of Wing Chun, a side-on pose with the forward foot turned slightly in towards the body and the back foot held at 45 degrees to the median line of the body.

t'an-tien (Cant: *tandim*) According to traditional Chinese theory, an area of the body located about 3 inches beneath the navel and another 2 inches within the body; the psychic or energy center akin to a Yogic chakra, which produces and stores the vital energy (*chi*) of the body. This energy can be directed against an opponent with the proper training.

taun dao A butterfly-knife action analogous to the *taun sao*, using the blunt edge of the blade to deflect a weapon and slow it down, so that it sticks to the blade and can be trapped and locked by the ear of the knife.

taun sao The asking-hand of Wing Chun, a straight thrusting-hand move used to deflect punches.

til gwon A pole technique similar to the *til sao* action in the *Sil Lum Tao*, used either to lift a weapon or to strike an opponent from the ground up. It is performed in the *dil mah* stance.

til sao A defensive lifting deflection designed for counter-attacking a punch with a grappling hand move.

tor sao The Wing Chun *tor sao* is really a modified *fook sao* with the fingers facing downward.

Wing Chun/Wing Tsun A non-traditional Chinese martial art that is highly regarded as an effective self-defense system. It is said to have been invented by a nun named Ng Mui, one of the only five survivors of the total destruction of the original Shaolin Temple. Legend has it that Ng Mui traveled to Futshan province, where she developed her own fighting style and passed it on to her best disciple, the daughter of another student, bean-curd maker Yim San Sohk, whose given name was Wing Chun (Beautiful Spring).

wooden-dummy A symbolic training tool allowing realistic powerful applications of striking techniques. It consists of a thick round post mounted on a supporting frame that allows the post to vibrate to some degree when struck. From the top part of the dummy, two smooth arms protrude and another single arm protrudes from the middle. The arms represent high- and middle-range attacks. There is also a forward leg with a bend in it which represents the knee of the forward leg. The lower stem of the dummy represents the back leg.

wu sao A defensive hand move known as worshiping the Buddha.

yin/yang According to Chinese cosmology, the two basic principles of the universe, which are both opposite to each other but complementary at the same time. Yang is characterized by things that are positive, active, and male; yin, by things that are negative, passive, and female.

yut ge dao The number one knife skill, is a knife defense where the knives are held so that the end of each guard touches, and the blades are in line with each other, facing the opponent. The point of this move is to create a larger blocking area.